OUTRAGEOUS POEMS

KRUNCHIE KILLEEN

The Outrageous Poems of Krunchie Killeen

Published by the Author, 3rd Edition, 2017
First published (Kalvagh Books) 2010

(Some of the poems were previously distributed, in manuscript or printed versions, or on the Internet, at various times since about 1959, as individual poems or in broadsheets or newspapers or digital book).

© Proinnsias Ó Cillín 1959 - 2017
All rights reserved.

ISBN-13:
978-1548093228

ISBN-10:
154809322X

Author's email address: KrunchieKilleen@gmail.com

Author's Web Site: www.killeens.info
and https://killeensinfo.blogspot.ie/

Printed by CreateSpace, an Amazon.com Company

Paperback version available on Amazon and other online stores

Ebook version available on Kindle

The Outrageous Poems of Krunchie Killeen

PREFACE TO THE 3RD EDITION

Many readers of these Outrageous Poems have started at the beginning of the book and read right through to the end, often in one sitting. Unusual for a book of poetry, this is as I would wish, for I would hope that every one of the poems is found to be entertaining, and I have arranged them to give a natural flow from one poem to the next.

I started writing poems when I was a child of seven, and quickly found that, to capture my audience, a poem had to be outrageous or comical. The attention of the audience has to be arrested by the first line of a poem, and every stanza after that must be moulded so as to hold that attention.

Naughty words are sometimes used by me for dramatic effect, but the content is not adult but amusing. Since I have grown old along with my audience, some topics are, of course, beyond the understanding of children.

Humour can be misunderstood, and one reader thought "The Miniskirt" was denigrating of women. It is not. It is a skit on the preachers and o-so-correct gentlemen who think that their "bad" sexual thoughts are caused by female immodesty, rather than by testosterone!

I laugh at myself, as well as taking a swipe at some outlandish repressive values I inherited as an Irish, twentieth century, Catholic.

Eleven additional poems have been added to this edition, interspersed through the rest. A few clerical and minor changes have been made to the others.

The Outrageous Poems of Krunchie Killeen

JUNIRA NATIONS

In a pub one night,
'Twas quite amazin';
I underwent
A transformation.

The music blared;
The people sang.
The spirit moved me;
Up I sprang.

I sang great songs
With all my neighbours,
Waving hands
And voicing quavers.

I thought no singer
In the town
Could make more musi-
cal a sound.

A smile spread out
Across my face.
By dad! I was
A happy case.

The Outrageous Poems of Krunchie Killeen

A quiet person
Up to now,
Totally
Transformed, I vow.

And, as the pub
Was spilling out,
Knowledge I
Began to spout.

I delivered
Wondrous wisdom,
Compelling every
One to listen.

All of a rush
I had the answers
To all the problems
Of the planet.

Quick, guys, call
Junira Nations:
They oughta hear
Our Krunchie spakin'.

The Outrageous Poems of Krunchie Killeen

TIT SHAKING

There was a fad in some Dublin pubs for ladies to expose their breasts, late on in the night, and do a bit of jolly tit-shaking. Great gas, except when it's your mother doing the thing. It is a bit of a skill, involving muscle movement from the knees up.

In this drinking place,
When the hour is getting late,
And we're all in a merry state,
You may see some tits a' shaking.
The music blares, nya nya,
Then off will come a bra,
And, bejasus, there's your ma
On her feet with tits a' shaking.

    No! No! Not now, ma!
    No! No! Not now, ma!
    No! No! Not now, ma!
    O No! Not now, ma!

So, ladies, seize this op,
Right now, remove your top,
Then let your lacy brassiere drop:
Let's see those tits a' shaking.

    No! No! Not now, ma!
    No! No! Not now, ma!
    No! No! Not now, ma!
    O No! Not now, ma!

The Outrageous Poems of Krunchie Killeen

We'll have a competition here,
The winner gets a pint of beer,
The loser gets another year
To practice her tit shaking.

    No! No! Not now, ma!
    No! No! Not now, ma!
    No! No! Not now, ma!
    O No! Not now, ma!

To fulfil a self-destructive wish,
Just tell a funky fellow this:
In a pub I recognised your bitch
In the shaking of her tits.

The Outrageous Poems of Krunchie Killeen

FEMALE MODES OF DRESS (OR THE MINISKIRT)

Every year there was a mission, where preachers visited the Parish to denounce sins of the flesh. Wednesday was ladies' night, when the womenfolk were harangued for their immodesty, including lipstick and mascara, the uplift bra, and any style that showed a bit of flesh. Gentlemen took the message on board, blaming women's immodesty for their recurring "bad" thoughts.

Is it any wonder
Sex inundates the nation,
When so many of our women
Are so provocative and brazen?

For, is it not their purpose
To make the fellows rise,
When sexy women show
 A bare display of thighs?

Is it not their aspiration
Men's passions to arouse,
When they flaunt a brassy bosom
Behind a bitsie blouse?

Yes! We've seen too often
In public places
Half-clothed hussies
Show their traces.

The Outrageous Poems of Krunchie Killeen

Not even knicker cover,
When breeze there is not,
On bus-stairs and escalator,
Where they display – the lot!

My eyes I keep averted,
But I know that there are scores
Of lads who've been corrupted
By such sights in city stores.

My eyes I keep averted,
Yet I cannot help but see,
And their flimsy little knickers
Cause turmoil inside of me.

My eyes I keep averted,
So, what damage must be done
To those dirty, sexy, bowsies,
Who peek and glare for fun!

So, brothers, let's take action.
This immodesty must stop!
Let each of us preach morality
Unto his own mot.

Yes! Unto your own mot!
And your women folk most near!

The Outrageous Poems of Krunchie Killeen

It is high time, gentlemen,
For us to make a stand
Against this flood of immodesty
That sweeps across the land.

Let us call upon the government
To take action to suppress
For once and all certain
Female modes of dress.

No more allow lithe ladies
Lure lads into sin
By display of any length of leg
At all, above the shin.

Let's call upon the Government
To ban revealing slits
And any styles that emphasise
Buttocks, thighs or tits.

Yes! Ban revealing slits,
And be ever on alert
To pre-empt every attempt
To revive the mini-skirt.

That shameful style of dress,
High above the knees, -
Not even knicker cover
In a little breeze!

The Outrageous Poems of Krunchie Killeen

Advise your sexy sisters
To wear more modest gear.

Let's tolerate no more
Our mothers and our aunts
To be prancing round the town
In those horrible hot pants.

Let's bid them search the attic
For the bloomers granny wore:
Cause them cover up their bodies
As in moral days of yore.

CAT

Someone saw a pussycat
And lured her to my door
With a bowl of breakfast milk,
And she came back for more.

She was a lovely creature
With soft and cuddly fur
That anyone who saw her
Could not but adore.

And she had admirers
Of her own ilk
With whom she soon was wont to
Share my breakfast milk.

But someone will regret it
When next she sees my face,
For the smell of cats' Malacca
Is all around the place.

CATERPILLAR

A little caterpillar
Crept out of the grass
Onto a concrete path
Where many humans pass.

A little caterpillar,
O, unlucky day!
Came from the insect world
Into the Humans' way.

A tiny caterpillar
Mid many mighty feet;
A frightened caterpillar
Making slow retreat.

A vibrant caterpillar
Just here before was found;
But now a yellow spatter
Is all that marks the ground.

PADDY BALONEY

This is a reconstruction of my very first poem, written when I was seven. The original was lost, because I tore it up in disappointment when my jovial classmate, the subject of the poem, said it was rubbish. It did not occur to me that his judgment of the poem's literary merit would be adversely affected by the fact that I called him "Paddy Baloney" and criticised the game he had created.

I'll tell you a story
About Paddy Baloney,
Who sits beside me in school.

He's very barmy;
He's got an army
Drawn on paper with pencil and rule.

If you sit down beside him,
You'll have to fight him,
With your own pencilled army, of course.

The game is a fiddle:
You must march down the middle,
So Paddy can outflank your force.

If you protest,
(I do not jest),
Paddy will insist it's the rule.

The Outrageous Poems of Krunchie Killeen

Whatever the weather,
Paddy's the winner,
And his foe is always the fool.

WRITING ABOUT YOU

I thought about this after doing a Bloomsday reading. Some of James Joyce's contemporaries were concerned with how their characters were maligned in Joyce's writings. But Joyce wrote fiction: he had free right and scope to mould his persona, even when inspired by living persons, into whatever character he wished. A fictional character does not purport to be a copy of a real person.

When I put you in my writing,
Let's be clear.
Out there, you are you,
Not in here.

In here you are a figment
Of my mind,
To muck about and rearrange
As I'm inclined.

You are nothing to my mind
But modelling clay
To mould and shape
In whatever way.

When I make you villain,
That is not absurd,
Even if you are hero
In your world.

The Outrageous Poems of Krunchie Killeen

And if I make you paragon,
Don't boast:
I can re-shape any shit
Into a rose.

GARDEN OF FLOWERS

A garden full of flowers:
So beautiful to see!
There I'd spend many hours
Beneath the flowering tree.

A garden full of blooms
Tossing their heads with glee,
A bird with merry tunes
High up in a tree.

A garden of blossoms bright
In beautiful array.
So now I don't give a shite.
It has blown my cares away.

CHRISTMAS WHEN

At some stage, an awakening body brings a re-appraisal of the universe of childhood.

Do you remember Christmas when
You were a few years past the age of ten
And Santa Claus had lost his spell
And magic: it was fading?

And big guys left your sister home
And kissed and mauled her by the door
While you lay in your bed alone
Quietly masturbating?

And up jumped Saint Peter, inside your head.
With wrath and ire he sternly said:
"You will regret this when you are dead
And in the arms of Satan."

 And Satan slipped in with a smile,
Saying, "Friend, fulfil what you desire;
Then come and sit down in my fire,
Until your arse be aching."

And then a bomb burst in your tool
And your tummy became a sea of gruel,
All of which began to give to Yule
A new interpretation.

The Outrageous Poems of Krunchie Killeen

GANDHI'S KNELL

At school, we, in good humour, imagined our teachers dead. Our science teacher, Brother Edward Laffan, nicknamed "Gandhi," was very much alive when I circulated this epitaph. "Beak" was our word for the principal teacher, nicknamed "Biffo," and "Pancho" was the nick-name of our form-master.

Here he died, where once he stood
Behind his mighty bench of wood,
Where golden crystals once showered down
And pen-knives turned a golden brown.

Here, from Winchester quarts,
He poured out acids, poured out salts.
Here the tears began to flow,
When we saw poor Gandhi go.

Then Handy stood, and said, said he:
"Never a hard word he said to me"
He tried to speak, but woe prevailed,
And Handy, like us all, just wailed.

And tears came streaming from his eyes,
And from the eyes of all the boys,
Until a mighty flood arose
That swept Beak Biffo off his toes.

The Outrageous Poems of Krunchie Killeen

Then Pancho, he came running round,
With his two feet upon the ground.
"Half day, Half day!" is what he cried,
The day that Gandhi died.

The Outrageous Poems of Krunchie Killeen

THE WITCH

A poem that came into my head, at sixteen years of age, as I tossed and turned in bed one stormy night! Full of imagery, I guess the great giants are the people holding power over me, the mighty river is the river of life, the vast halls the colleges, schools, courts, police stations, parliament buildings and other edifices of authority and the maidens, bright and dark, the sexual snares lying in wait for me.

Where great giants gather
For colloquy in vast halls,
And hang their mighty spears
From ropes around the walls;

And great, golden rivers
Rush forever to the sea,
Mid rugged hills, grey rocks
And wild scenery;

In a sudden flowery valley,
Where sweet scents filled the air,
There stood a mighty mansion
Where lived eight sisters fair.

One upon a thorn tree
Forever did repose,
But the other seven sisters
The softest luxury chose.

The Outrageous Poems of Krunchie Killeen

The gold, gleaming in the river,
Matched their golden hair,
As the seven sisters played
In languid leisure there.

But, when a wizard bade them
To wish inside their head,
They wished, each, for a handsome man
With whom to share her bed.

Just then, as if by magic,
Seven handsome lads appeared
Galloping round the birch wood
That formed their magic screen.

The sparks flew from the horses hooves
As the gallant lads drew nigher,
And, in the seven sisters' hearts
There grew a torrent of desire.

They stopped; they smiled; their eyes were caught
In the golden hair:
Seven smiling faces
That were oh! So fair!

They sniffed the scent of roses
And gazed the glen around

The Outrageous Poems of Krunchie Killeen

To where the deepest, dark woods
Cast shadows on the ground.

Down a dim-lit stairway,
By a magic well,
They saw the fairest face
That one can ever tell.

Her hair was oh! So dark!
As dark as ripest sloe.
Her skin was oh! So white!
Nor whiter is the snow.

Her eyes were deep and witching,
A deep and witching grey;
And each swore that he would be her slave
And follow her alway.

There was a flowery valley,
But the flowers are dead and gone,
And, from the deepest, dark wood,
There comes a mournful song.

Some old, old men are moaning
Down by the thorny tree;
They'll mourn and mourn forever
Into eternity.

The Outrageous Poems of Krunchie Killeen

And the giants in their mighty halls
Shall hearken to their calling,
Where the great and golden waters
Are forever falling;

For the witch upon the thorn tree
Has weaved her spell of woe;
Has sapped their strength, has taken flight;
Aye, to the sky has flown.

And every night I hear her
When the wind is blowing loud,
For her shrill laugh re-echoes
From the deepest, dark cloud;

And I know that she will laugh,
And laugh until she burst,
For the hearts she has broken,
The people she cursed.

COLM CILLE AT LOCH NESS

This poem mixes stories of Saint Colm Cille, (or Columba), who is credited with taming the Loch Ness Monster. He is said to have lived from 521 to 597, except that he did not die for years after that date, writing prophecies in old age. His hagiographers gave him this early death, because they thought 75 was a good age to die, in case the Saint might be thought of as a senile old man. "Krumm" is the Celtic God, Crom Cruach, to whom selfish people could turn for unfair advantage. It was not considered correct for Christians to pray for advantage over others. (The) Donegal (branch of the Royal Family) succeeded in the contest mentioned in the poem, a bloody battle inspired by Colm, who felt that the incumbent Meath king had been unjust in some of his actions. Colm's monasteries were at the forefront of the horticulture of the day, and cultivated several herbs, including St. John's Wort, which continues to be valued in these Islands, though banned now for sale in Irish health-food shops.

At a contest between Donegal and Meath,
The saint prayed, "Let Donegal succeed."
He should have prayed, "Thy Will be done."
His prayer rose not to Christ, but Krumm.

To atone for his sinful prayer, so vile,
He threw his life into exile,
To spread the loving Word of God
Far away from his native sod.

The Outrageous Poems of Krunchie Killeen

Coming to Loch Ness, he found
 A beast spreading terror all around.
He called the monster from the bay,
Until, prostate at his feet, it lay.

Then he issued this stern command:
"Be at peace; cause no more harm."
And ever since that very day,
Men sail safely across Ness Bay.

Then the saint strode across the land
Bringing his word of peace to man.
In response, the Scots gave up their arms
And, living in peace, caused no more harm.

To make sure
That so they'd stay,
He fed them John's Wort
Every day.

FRANKIE WANKIE

Every Francis is, at some stage, called "Frankie Wankie," entirely without malice. It is, let me make clear, with humour that I take exception to the moniker. Wasting one's seed, let me add, is a reference to the Catholic denouncement of any sperm-spillage outside of a valid act of intercourse within marriage.

Frankie Wankie is not my name.
Would you call me Krunchie, please, for shame!
And explain what is it; what's your game,
That you called me Frankie Wankie?

I have never wanked and that's for sure,
Except once or twice when immature.
I'd rather ride a riddled whore
Than waste my seed a' wanking.

All the ladies know that I am great
Everywhere I go they line up and wait,
Each one wishing with me to mate,
So, I have no need of wanking.

And every night, when I hit the sack,
My hands are tied behind my back.
Ipso facto: it's a proven fact,
They can't be used for wanking.

The Outrageous Poems of Krunchie Killeen

If the fences now you wish to mend,
And you want once more to be my friend,
Solemnly you must agree
Not to call me Frankie Wankie.

APPROACHING TWENTY

I have lived.
But soon, I see, I will have reached
The crabby old age of twenty,
Whence forth I shall frown
On all those sweet enjoyments
Which made life dear,
And crawl
From day to day with toil
Like all old men.

Heyday, thou art done!
Inevitable age will soon possess my bones,
Thoughts dull and sombre
Take refuge in my mind,
For no man can escape
The clawing clutch of time.

Soon, I'll point my finger at the teens
And call them "Crazy, Mixed Up,"
As the Twenties of my day did me,
And spend all the rest of my existence
Crawling out.

TWENTY-ONE (PUT YOUR MINISKIRT ON)

Hey there, you fine thing, now you're twenty one,
Just go and put your miniskirt on;
Tart up your face and put on a false tan
And go to the disco and bring home a man.

Go on now, get your man;
Go on now, get your man;
Go on now, get your man,
Get your man, get your man.

Alas and alack, our youth is soon gone.
It's only one year that you'll be twenty one.
Therefore, don't dawdle; don't let the year pass:
Start shaking your tits and start wiggling your ass.

Go on now, get your man;
Go on now, get your man;
Go on now, get your man,
Get your man, get your man.

Go do it, go do it; but, please, don't delay.
Down in the disco, your charms please display.
Of all the men there, just pick one from the pool;
Then hook him, and pull him and haul home the fool.

The Outrageous Poems of Krunchie Killeen

Go on now, get your man;
Go on now, get your man;
Go on now, get your man,
Get your man, get your man.

So I'm saying to you, now that you're twenty one,
You should just go put your miniskirt on.
And tart up yourself as well as you can
And get down to the disco and bring home a man.

The Outrageous Poems of Krunchie Killeen

THE BOURGEOISIE

"Comrades" and "Workers' Party," I found, were just
as provocative as "Tits" and "Knickers."

Ah, Comrades, listen to what I say:
I got a message for you today:
This country will never be truly free,
Till we eliminate the Bourgeoisie,

The profiteers, the middlemen,
The property speculators.
They are eating up the earnings
Of you and me, like ravenous alligators.

The working man has been betrayed
By the bankers and the money trade,
And politicians who sponsor greed
And bolster the power of the Bourgeoisie,

The profiteers, the middlemen,
The property speculators,
Who are eating up the earnings
Of you and me, like ravenous alligators.

So, Comrades, come out and strike the blow;
For the Workers' Party cast your vote:
Let Honesty, Courage and Integrity
Replace the culture of the Bourgeoisie,

The profiteers, the middlemen,
The property speculators,
Who are eating up the earnings
Of you and me, like ravenous alligators.

MY LOVE BITES

Dear Agony, this letter said,
My boyfriend does strange things in bed.
I fear it is a mortal sin;
He never puts his organ in;
My cheek and chin he tends to peck,
Then sinks his teeth into my neck.

Miss Column pondered and then wrote:
This may be the kind of bloke,
Old fashioned, (though I dearly doubt),
Who thinks to keep his organ out
Is, indeed, less of a sin
Than if he put said organ in.

But you have given few details;
Perhaps he really tries but fails:
Could it be that you are tight or small,
Or that he has no balls at all.
Have you verified, - with your hand,-
That he is truly as God planned?

When he bites, does he draw blood,
Then smack his lips and say, "That's Good!"
And, when he raises up his head,
Do his mouth corners dribble red?
And do you shiver and near expire?
Yes, is your boyfriend a Vampire?

The Outrageous Poems of Krunchie Killeen

If so, it is your Virgin Blood
He goes for, as his Wonder Food.
As the matter, then, rests on a thin piece of tissue,
Your milkman can readily resolve the issue.
If, after the milkman, boyfriend still bites,
He's not a vampire, and you're all right.

But, if you are a moral conservative,
Here's the advice that I must give:
At night by your bedside place
Some Holy Water and a stake,
And, as he pecks your cheek or chin,
Pour the water over him.

If this shatters his desire
And makes him shout, "Christ, I'm on fire,"
Grab the stake, and with one dart,
Drive it through his demon heart.
Drop his body off the Cliffs of Moher,
And then, dear Mary, your problem's over.

Yet one thing still occurs to me
Of some importance, you'll agree.
You did not say if you enjoy
This peck-and-bite love of your boy.
If so, forget that other crap
And go on bedding with your chap.

The Outrageous Poems of Krunchie Killeen

A diet of good, wholesome food
To keep up your supply of Virgin blood;
Keep your milkman outside the gate;
Don't bother with Holy Water or stake;
Whether or not he's a foul Vampire,
Let him peck away to his heart's desire.

TYPING SECTION

I often get a quiet erection,
When I visit Typing Section.

When I walk in, it blows my wits
Confronting such a show of tits
In miscellaneous shape and size,
And all conducive to my eyes.

There is no better boob selection
Anywhere than Typing Section.

When I walk in what sparkling eyes,
What lively banter, flashing smiles!
And, when I have again walked out,
No doubt it's me they talk about.

It seems the girls in Typing Section
Welcome men and male attention.

When I walk in, at once the scent
Of musk and perfume they present
Makes my hormones spring to action,
Enveloping me in their attraction.

I often get quite an erection
When I visit Typing Section.

The Outrageous Poems of Krunchie Killeen

JOAN MAGUIRE

(From, and to the air of, the song in Irish, "Siún Ní Dhuibhir")

Early this morning I left for the fair in Boyle.
I met a fine lady who threw me a friendly smile.
I sat down beside her to chat for a little while,
And I spent all my money there drinking with Joan Maguire.

O, Joan Maguire, you've ruined my life, you bitch.
You captured my heart, yet yielded me ne'er a kiss.
When I was spendin' your attention was warm and rich;
When my pocket was empty, I found I was promptly ditched.

Now here I am in this town of Boyle forlorn,
Feeling so foolish, I wish that I ne'er was born.
Can't do my duty: my money is spent and gone.
When I try to stand up, I'm so drunk that again I fall.

My curse on this town with its women so wild and free.
My curse on the townies who trick country boys like me.
My curse on my parents for rearing such a blithering fool,
And my twenty five curses upon my misguided tool.

The Outrageous Poems of Krunchie Killeen

O, Joan Maguire, I dream of you day and night,
Your friendly smile, your eyes sparkling with delight.
Though you're a rogue, I long for your soft caress,
My arms to enfold you and hold you close to my
    breast.

The Outrageous Poems of Krunchie Killeen

TRAIN TO HELL

We have an idea that Ireland is an island of saints, (whatever about the scholars). Perhaps, however, we are mistaken and other nationalities, with their liberalism, are more acceptable to God.

I took a Train to Heaven:
But Oh! What an awful smell,
For on the opposite platform
Was a Train that was bound for Hell.

As we waited at the station,
I had a look inside the other,
To see what sort of scum it carried;
But was I surprised, dear mother.

For not a foreign face I found,
Nor signs of criminality.
All were good-living Irish folk,
The cream of the Sodality.

Through an open window,
I asked what had gone wrong,
And a white-haired Irish mother
Answered for that throng.

"Son, weren't we all waiting
At the Pearly Gates,
And Himself viewing the multitudes
From a hundred states.

The Outrageous Poems of Krunchie Killeen

He addressed the British wankers
And said "That's no great sin,
And, if you've nothing else to declare,
Ye may walk right in."

Next, he took a crowd of French:
"Vous all had love affairs.
But, sure love's a blessing,
So you're welcome, folk, upstairs."

And he took a crowd of yanks,
Who had thrown aside their wives.
"Come in, he said: at least
You loved for a little while."

He took in robbers and rapists
And murderers as well,
Black folks, yellow and red folks:
Was there no one, then, for Hell?

As he let in harlots and lechers
And whiskey-swilling nasties,
We sodality folk were thinking
That this is a disaster.

As we welled with indignation,
He must have heard our mutters,
For He turned and said in an off-hand way:
"And to Hell with the begrudgers."

The Outrageous Poems of Krunchie Killeen

Well, as the train for Hell sped off,
I stepped down from my train,
And I'll ponder well this mystery
Before I set out again.

RAFTERY THE POET

Inspired by Anthony Raftery's line "Ag seinm ceoil do phócaí follamha," ("Playing music to empty pockets"), this poem depicts Raftery as a blind, drunken, beggar, scrounging pennies from pub to pub. In reality, he was quite successful as a public entertainer, playing the violin as well as singing and reciting poetry, and earning a reasonable living from this profession. Though he talks of wandering around the country, he stuck mostly to East Galway where he had a few well-paying haunts.

He was nought but a blind beggar-poet,
Cadging a drink when he could,
Getting pennies for performing his verses,
Groping drunkenly at girls in the pub.

His poems were a blind beggar's verses,
Though they lived on, bringing him fame.
Gentle folk dreaded his table,
And avoided his presence like plague.

It was fine to stand at a distance,
Enjoying the flow of his words,
But, did you want to share in his drinking,
Till both you and he slumped to the boards?

Of course, he had plenty companions,
Each one as bad as the next,
Who helped him to drink all his pennies,
While enjoying his rhymes and his verse.

The Outrageous Poems of Krunchie Killeen

There were nights filled with singing and music,
When Raftery basked in applause,
And drank his fill of strong whiskey,
Welcoming the oblivion this brought.

Not long in one place could he linger,
For the pennies would soon all dry up.
Off he went with his stick and his knapsack,
To find another town and a pub.

He often mused on the misfortune
That one's time and one's place could bring,
For poets of previous generations
Lived rich lives in the courts of the kings.

The kings were long gone from Ireland,
And gowls now ruled in their place,
And it was only peasants now sponsored
The literature of his race.

The Outrageous Poems of Krunchie Killeen

BRIAN BORU'S FEASTING

The feasting at Kincora,
In the court of Brian Boru,
Was lavish in its splendour
And splendid through and through.

The Chieftains of all Ireland
To this feasting came,-
Where you would also find
The leading Norse and Dane.

Lavish were the quantities
And quality of the food,
Along with wines and spirits
To jolly up the mood.

No glass was ever empty,
No platter ever bare,
But every guest was offered
His fill of the finest fare.

In keeping with kingly custom,
Brian ordered that every feast
Be furnished with all greens and fruits
And no less than seven meats.

As well as wines from Europe,
He served red, rural ale,

The Outrageous Poems of Krunchie Killeen

And a yellow beer from Dublin,
People were to call "the Pale."

And, here, Brian showed his genius,
For, when all had feasted well,
He bade the finest women
Show their legs to the foreign men.

Around his feasting table
Many marriages were made,
As beautiful Irish women
Cajoled the Norse and Danes.

The fathers of these Norse and Danes
By force had taken brides.
Now the feasting table
Was the start of love's alliance.

And, thus, Brian demonstrated
There was no need for war.
Our girls were wild for Viking men,
But under Irish law.

And prosperity was there for all
By means of peaceful trade,
Making totally pointless
All the wars and raids.

The Outrageous Poems of Krunchie Killeen

And it was Brian's plan for peace
That would win him great renown,
Were it not that the king of Leinster
Conspired to bring him down.

HIMALAYAN LONGEVITY

Longevity of 150 years is claimed for people who live in the high Himalayas, including Tibet, Georgia, Hunza, Sherpa, Nepal and Kashmir. There are no records, however, to prove the claims. The oldest person on record is Jeanne Calment who died in 1999 aged 122 and 5 months and enjoyed chocolate and port, and smoked up to age 117.

High up in the Himalayas
They Live a hundred and fifty years
And women of over a hundred
Still look like Britney Spears.

They don't drink coca-cola
Or eat processed foods at all,
But only stuff they grow themselves,
Which they like to gobble raw.

And, when they consume an apricot,
They eat the kernel too,
Cracking open the little nut,
To enjoy a bitter chew.

The medicines that they take
To sustain them through the years
Are the products of the mountainside
They've used four thousand years.

Their longevity is recognised
In travellers' tale and song,

The Outrageous Poems of Krunchie Killeen

But they don't have any certificates
To prove that they were born.

So in the Book of Records
They are not acknowledged there,
And the record goes to a French girl
Of a hundred and twenty two years.

But, if this French girl, Jeanne Calment,
Had climbed hills every day,
And abstained from fags and port and sugar,
She would still be alive today.

So, take up mountain walking,
And start a veggy plot
And live on seeds and roots and greens
And the nuts of apricots.

The Outrageous Poems of Krunchie Killeen

LILY WHITE BREAST

A song to a traditional Irish template, in the air of *Bríd Óg Ní Mháille.*

With each breath of my breathing
Of you I'm surely dreaming,
For, my heart and my mind,
They are never at rest.
As distracted forth I sally,
I am blind to hill and valley,
For all I see before me
Is your lily-white breast.

O God, your lily-white breast!

Obsessed with my love's beauty
I neglect my chores and duty.
The rose and the lily
In her cheeks do contest.
A delicate rose petal
Is the lip that tests my metal,
And the rose, it forms a crown
On her lily-white breast.

O God, her lily-white breast!

I've forsaken my own father,
I've forsaken my mother;
I've forsaken my brother

The Outrageous Poems of Krunchie Killeen

And all of the rest.
By her charms I am so taken,
My very God I have forsaken;
And it's all for the sake of
Her lily-white breast.

O God, her lily-white breast!

You people of great learning
Know how Paris fought for Helen.
Well, I understand the passion
With which he was possessed.
For I'd truly drive a skewer
Through the heart of any boor
Who would try to prise my hand from
Her lily-white breast.

Yes, I'd truly drive a skewer
Through the heart of any boor
Who would try to prise my hand from
Her lily-white breast.

The Outrageous Poems of Krunchie Killeen

RETIREMENT SONG

They expect you to say you have mixed feelings about leaving, and that you will miss them all. Instead, give them this. Air: Vincent Campbell's Mazurka.

Now I'm Leaving, I'm glad to go.
Will I miss you? No!
Will I miss you? No!
Now I'm Leaving, I'm glad to go.
Will I miss you all?
That's No.

I am going to have a better time.
Very soon all of this be far behind.
I assure you, you won't be on my mind.
Now I'm leaving, I'm glad to go.

Now I'm Leaving, I'm glad to go.
Will I miss you? No!
Will I miss you? No!
Now I'm Leaving, I'm glad to go.
Will I miss you all?
That's No.

I have cleared all the rubbish from my desk.
I am heading away out to the west.
I'll be greeting the sunrise and sunsets.
Now I'm leaving, I'm glad to go.

The Outrageous Poems of Krunchie Killeen

Now I'm Leaving, I'm glad to go.
Will I miss you? No!
Will I miss you? No!
Now I'm Leaving, I'm glad to go.
Will I miss you all?
That's No.

No more cursing the traffic in the morn.
No more seething in the office when it's warm.
No more beating the deadlines at the dawn.
Now I'm leaving, I'm glad to go.

Now I'm Leaving, I'm glad to go.
Will I miss you? No!
Will I miss you? No!
Now I'm Leaving, I'm glad to go.
Will I miss you all?
That's No.

Now I'll wheel out the keyboard to the room
And you'll hear me bash out a happy tune
And it's mighty the singing I'll be doin';
Now I'm leaving, I'm glad to go.

Now I'm Leaving, I'm glad to go.
Will I miss you? No!
Will I miss you? No!
Now I'm Leaving, I'm glad to go.
Will I miss you all? That's No.

THE HERO

An overwhelming force against him plied.
He fired a shot and jumped to cover. Then,
Leaping out, he clobbered two armed men
And hooked their captured weapons to his side.

With a mighty shout he charged their startled rank.
A grenade he threw to silence their big gun.
Before they could take aim at him he'd run
Through a door into a passage dark and dank.

Racing down this tunnel, he neared his prize,
The dread dictator who must be overthrown.
Shattering the palace door, he faced him all alone,
Flinching there before his steady eyes.

Poised now on the very verge of victory,-
His mum comes out and calls him in for tea.

The Outrageous Poems of Krunchie Killeen

STATUE

The typical Irish Catholic home of the mid 20th Century was decorated with religious reproductions, to which company, American president John F Kennedy was an acceptable addition. The emergence of secular art in modern homes was seen by some conservatives as a betrayal of the wholesome values of the past. I wrote the poem on arrival at a house-warming party in Galway in the 1960s to find a Venus statue in the hallway.

In the naked nude it stands,
A Venus statue without hands.
Woe, woe, woe; yes, woe is me!
It is a sinful sight to see.

It is a sight would make you shiver,
So dry your throat, you'd drink a river.
But 'tis not thoughts of drink you'd think,
But thoughts from which Christians ought to shrink.

Fault not yourself; those thoughts can't lie,
While those taunting tits assault your eye.
Shameful, naked, taunting tits!
What an awful thing it is

To have such a statue in the hallway
Of a Christian home in Galway!
Christian home! Is it? Where you won't see
Pictured pope, saint, or John F. Kennedy!

The Outrageous Poems of Krunchie Killeen

It brings, it brings tears to my eyes;
For what sort of morals does it symbolise?
Rotten Morals! Aye, it's plain to see
We've entered the permissive society;

Immodesty engulfs the nation
And immorality is raging.

WORMS

Worms and creepy things abound
In my garden, crawling round.
And, when the ground is sodden through,
Up they come for all to view.

Turn a stone and they surprise us
In their many shapes and sizes.
Healthy brown worms, bright with slime,
These I like, but have no time

For those sickly greens or yellows,
Or those lively, wiry, rusty fellows
Of many feet, who eat my tubers,
Occasioning in me Most Violent Humours;

For, when you splice them with your spade,
Both halves live that you have made,
And wriggle off into the clay
To gorge again another day

Upon whatever you have sown.
And you wonder why your flower has grown
So slow, and why its blooms
Are anaemic, sickly things, till soon

You dig it up, and then you see
Six hundred creatures wriggle free.

The Outrageous Poems of Krunchie Killeen

Sometimes, when you sit at table
To eat a feed, if you are able,

Of lettuce and other garden greens,
You think you've of a sudden seen
Something stir upon your plate.
You look again to see a great,

Big, slimy, yellow snail
Which even your wife's wily washing failed
To dislodge from the leaf
You nearly had between your teeth.

Green worms, grey worms, red worms, blue,
How I hate the lot of you.
If I find you in my way,
I'll make a mash of you for play.

SPARE A THOUGHT

Spare a thought for wriggly worms
Round your garden creeping.
Remember, friend, that when you dig,
You leave worm widows weeping.

They are friendly little things.
They do not sting or bite you.
In fact, indeed, I cannot think
Of any harm they might do.

But they do a lot of good,
If you leave them to it.
For they will dig your plot for you,
As they tunnel through it.

But do you give them half a chance?
Indeed, I see you do not.
You gardening enthusiasts
Are, indeed, a cruel lot.

You wield your spades with energy;
You chop and lacerate them.
You do not seem to care a whit
To what woes you fate them.

The Outrageous Poems of Krunchie Killeen

Please spare a thought for wriggly worms
Through the soft soil snaking;
Think a while, before you smile,
Of the happy homes you're breaking.

THE GREAT GOD PAN

Pan, in mythology, is a god, in the form of a great hunk of a man as far as the waist, but from there on down he takes the form of a goat. He roams around the countryside playing sweet music on his flute, and those who hear this music, particularly females, are filled with zest for life; it awakens their sensual nature.

The Great God Pan, when he plays his whistle,
Makes all the females that hear him bristle;
Quickens their pulse and, by the gallon,
Their glands secrete adrenaline.

As his gentle notes float down the valley,
Watch Mary prance, and Jane, and Sally;
See them cock their heads, and blush, and listen
For the Great God Pan on his whistle.

Bright-eyed, they throw a tentative smile
At any man within a mile,
Uplift their breasts and wag their bottom,
For Pan has put the longing on them.

'Tis Pan that drew that sensuous smile,
That eyelid flick for to beguile;
And, when they heave those sighs and moon,
'Tis the Great God Pan and his tune.

The Outrageous Poems of Krunchie Killeen

Then, what is it that women like the best?
Is it the guitar, the song, the verse?
'Tis not, for I'll tell you the very plain truth:
It's the Great God Pan, and the flute.

JIMMY LOVES MARY

Jimmy loves Mary a lot.
They tell me the word is "besot."
    To get him to wed,
    Did she hold a gun to his head?
The answer is clear: she did not.

She did it by womanly charms;
By cajoling and spinning him yarns;
    By dancing and dining,
    And boozing and wining,
And reclining at night in his arms.

The Outrageous Poems of Krunchie Killeen

BOOKS

I'll lay these wretched books,
Lay them aside for sure.
Just now for chronic boredom
I need an instant cure.

Enough of this damn swotting,
This reading, writing, blotting.
This instant I'll be trotting
Where there's drinking, crack and motting.

A place of dissipation
Shall be my destination,
Where drink and wild temptation
Will fire imagination.

Where no priest's preaching tongue
Between me and joy will come,
But girls all warm and young
Who to my beck will throng.

My black pint frothing cream,
And a girl as in a dream,
Her glassy eye agleam
With wicked woman's scheme.

The Outrageous Poems of Krunchie Killeen

IN SLATTERY'S

Where, in the late 1960s, I ran a folk club at which *The Pavees* – consisting of John Keenan Snr & Jnr, Paddy Keenan, Paul & George Furey and Mick Moriarty – were the resident group.

It's been some weeks since I've been here:
You may have wondered where I'd gone.
Well, I've been to London town,
A place renowned for crack and song.

A place renowned for pleasures, too,
Of another nature,
Like the blond I met in Soho,
A really glorious creature.

Her eyes were like two bright full moons;
Her lips were red as fire;
She said that for a ten-pound note
I could have my heart's desire.

I replied to her most gratefully,
And here's what I dared say:
"O, to be back home in Slattery's
And to hear the Pavees play."

They have these pubs in London town
That people call Beer Kellers,
Where the girls drink quarts of German beer
And literally throw themselves at the fellers.

The Outrageous Poems of Krunchie Killeen

And they sing those good old folksy songs
Like "Knees up, Mother Brown,"
And they stand up on the tables
And fling their legs around.

Well, I sang out like any man,
And here's what I did sing:
"O, to be back home in Slattery's,
Where the Pavees do their thing."

They have these shows in London town,
Where admission is not cheap,
Where the dancing girls take off their clothes
And throw them in a heap.

And sometimes they pretend they're shy,
And that they won't take off their drawers,
And the bowsies in the audience
Shout, "Off, off, get them off!"

Well, I shouted out like any man,
But this is what I roared:
"O, to be back home in Slattery's,
Where I wouldn't be so bored."

KRUNCHIE AND MELANIA

I asked an 86 year old man how he was. He replied: "Well, I'm still chasing women, but I can't keep up with them now."

Have you seen Melania?
Wherever is she gone,
With her yellow hair a flying
And her glitzy jumpsuit on?

I only want to be with her,
To hold her dainty hand,
And why she does not wait for me
I do not understand.

The reason I can't catch her
Is that she moves so quick;
But I keep hobbling after
Upon my walking stick.

If she doesn't like me,
That might be, I suppose,
That I have wrinkles on my forehead
And a wart upon my nose.

I'll rub cream into my forehead,
Until every wrinkle goes,
And have a surgeon cut the wart
Right off my knobbly nose.

The Outrageous Poems of Krunchie Killeen

So, when you see me coming
With a bandage on my face,
You'll know that I have suffered
For Melania's sake.

If you see Melania,
Please send her back to me.
I'll buy her lovely apple tart
And a pot of golden tea.

I'll go to the flower shop
And buy her a red, red rose,
Or, if she likes rare orchids,
I'll buy her some of those.

I'll buy her fine silk dresses
And ribbons for her hair,
And dress her like a fairy queen
And take her everywhere.

I'll take her to the theatre
And to the hub of every hub.
I'll even have her dine with me
At the Bankers' Club.

Me and Melania
As a couple will be nice, --
Her hair as fine as soft silk,
My beard like iron spikes.

The Outrageous Poems of Krunchie Killeen

Her soft skin the colours
Of the lily and the rose;
My face like wrinkled autumn leaves,
And my pink and purple nose.

Her face all bright and lively,
Her dazzling, snappy smile;
The expression of importance
And authority on mine.

O, madam fortune-teller,
Will I win my Wonder girl?
She'd prefer a younger man, sir,
With teeth as white as pearl.

Well, I'll take me to the dentist
And get my black teeth out,
And he'll fix me up a set of teeth
As fine as any youth's.

She'd prefer a younger man, sir,
With black and curly hair.
Well, I'll buy myself a black wig
And then be quite as fair.

When she sees me in my new wig
And white and shiny teeth,
She'll smile a smile for me then
And warmly me will greet.

The Outrageous Poems of Krunchie Killeen

Surely she will offer
A soft and gentle kiss!
Then she'll enjoy the prickles
Of my beard upon her lips.

She will be so filled with joy,
She'll shout to all the land,
"From this moment on, please note,
That Krunchie is my man."

I see a happy picture:
Me in my rocking chair
And Melania sitting by the fire
Combing her yellow hair.

With all the money in my bank
We'll live a life so grand,
Krunchie and Melania
Will be the envy of the land.

We'll have Champagne for breakfast,
For dinner and for tea,
And the best of beef and mutton
And salmon from the sea.

And every single day,
As Melania cooks my meals,
She'll tell me once again
How happy she feels.

The Outrageous Poems of Krunchie Killeen

And every single morning,
As Melania makes my bed,
She'll tell me she's so happy,
So happy that we're wed.

Before she cooks my breakfast,
As Melania sets the fire,
She'll let me know she loves me
And that I'm her heart's desire.

And every single noontime,
As Melania scrubs the pots,
She'll let me know, of course,
That she loves me lots.

As she whizzes round our mansion
With her Hoover and her mop,
She'll tell me that her love for me
Will never, never, stop.

And every single evening,
As Melania pours the wine,
She'll let me know she loves me
And considers me divine.

Daily after dinner,
As she washes up,
I'll snore upon my rocking chair
Until it's time to sup.

WOMAN'S DESIRE

I am the opposite of woman's desire.
I fart and I belch by the fire.
   I'm scornful when questioned,
   Defensive, resentful;
But, at least, I am not a liar.

I am honest right down to a T.
You won't get fake news from me.
   If you ask are you fat,
   I'll say: "Yes, you are that;
It's a fact that's as plain as can be."

The Outrageous Poems of Krunchie Killeen

THE DA

You wonder why I look so sad,
So dishevelled and unshaved:
It's because my Daddy is a cripple
And my Mammy's in her grave.

Yes, my Daddy is a cripple
And a right contrary man,
And, when he has his Fits of Temper,
It's then I miss my Mam.

For she was very nimble
About her nursing job.
As soon as Da began to rage,
She'd belt him on the gob.

She was the most effective nurse
That you ever saw.
She hit him many times with force,
Yet never broke his jaw.

And, when she hit him once like that,
'Twas like a flow of Grace;
Da became relaxful
And Peace was on his face.

The Outrageous Poems of Krunchie Killeen

He often rested peacefully
For five long hours or more,
His head hung limply forward,
And not the slightest snore.

But now he rages all day long,
Complaining of his woes.
So, I've decided, once for all,
That my Daddy goes.

I know that I shall miss him,
For I truly love the Da.
I'll hit him with the hatchet,
The way I hit the Ma.

I know that they'll be happier
United up above,
And wait for me, all tenderly,
With familial love.

So, I'll sharpen up the hatchet,
And I'll ready make his grave,
And, the day before the funeral,
I'll clean myself and shave.

And all will be right tidy,
I won't make a mess of blood
Like when I killed the Mammy:
That would not be good.

The Outrageous Poems of Krunchie Killeen

Da was very jaded
After cleaning up that mess.
But, when I chop his head of,
I must mop up myself.

So, this time there will be no mess.
All will be right clean.
His head will go with one swift blow
O'er a sheet of polythene.

I'll wrap up in the polythene
The head, the trunk, the lot,
And bury them right neatly
Down by the cabbage plot.

I'll bury them right neatly
Down by the garden wall
Between his wife and four proud sons:
He truly loved them all.

He loved them; I loved them too.
I much regret their deaths.
But they all got what they deserved;
Each was, in his way, a pest.

But the biggest pest survived the rest,
For that truly is the Da.
Now I'm filled with zest, I'll enjoy the best
Hatcheting him ... Ha haaaaaaa!

The Outrageous Poems of Krunchie Killeen

THE GREAT SIX - O

The great Six-O to me has come;
Another phase of life begun;
Family grown and duty done;
Pass on my mantle to my son;
      Fuck it!

Now my mind begins to dwell
On pleasures that I should know well,
But never knew, the truth to tell,
Or of which I only got the smell;
      Fuck it!

The many things I have not done,
Jumped from a plane, the Channel swum;
Olympic medals never won,
Nor in the Eurovision sung;
      Fuck it!

All the pleasures that I have missed;
All those girls I never kissed;
All the nights I could have been pissed;
Yes! All the temptations I did resist;
      Fuck it!

The Outrageous Poems of Krunchie Killeen

The time is short; it's running out.
Bring me another pint of stout.
And Girls, line up along the wall;
For Krunchie wants to ride yiz all:
       Hop to it!

MY GARDEN

A blaze of golden colour
Will delight the eye
Of all the massive multitudes
That pass my garden by.

Vigorous and healthy
Are the things my garden grows,
Unlike my careful neighbour's
Neat, neurotic rows.

My lawn grows strong and lusty
And never is shaved bare.
Unlike my neighbour's skinhead lawn,
There's form and contrast there.

And if my niggly neighbour
Finds cause there to complain,
What is that to me, sir?
I'll answer just the same:

My garden is magnificent
In nature's own design,
With its mass of mighty dock leaves
And golden dandelions.

GOOD MORNING

With a gentle "Good Morning" I wake her.
Her response is a grunt and a groan.
"Good Morning, my Darling", I whisper.
She mutters, "Just leave me alone."

"We've time for a ride, love, this morning!"
She answers, "Then go ride the cat!"
What makes this so heartless, of course, is the fact that
She knows that I would not do that.

So I lie on my back agitated, -
Once again she commences to snore, -
And I help your man stand by applying my hand,
While I dream a' Philomena next door.

SNOW WHITE

Snow White, when she grew up,
Became a wicked queen.
The mirror on the wall
Foreclosed her dream.

Grey hairs and wrinkles
Began to appear;
And her lovely smile
Transformed into a sneer.

"O no," she exclaimed,
"This person that I see
Is my cruel stepmother:
It's not me!"

The impact of this insight
Made her cry,
For she knew that she could now
Lash out and destroy

The young princesses
Who would take her place
To win the hearts of men
With fresh young face.

The Outrageous Poems of Krunchie Killeen

And, knowing that she was
Capable of this thought,
She dressed up
In a lavish dress she'd bought.

VACANT MOOD

Unlike that other poet,
When on a couch I lie,
It is not golden daffodils
That flash before my inward eye.

It is not golden daffodils;
It's brazen birds, so rude.
But, from this moment, I'm resolved:
No more shall they intrude.

Should sexy scenes present themselves
Across the window of my mind,
Decisively; yes, like a flash,
Down will crash the roller blind.

I'll call to mind great hurling matches,
Sportsmen battling for a ball.
Though heads be split and knuckles shattered,
Here, there's no place for sex at all.

But no! O no! How can it be?
What show of harlotry is this?
The field's aswarm with wicked women,
Skirts blowing high and bobbing tits.

The Outrageous Poems of Krunchie Killeen

Away, away from these tormentors,
To scenes of calm and rest I'll turn;
In sweet solitude I'll see me lie
At ease, beneath a golden sun.

Good grief! And is there no relief?
Where're I turn, must they intrude?
For, stretched out on the sand around me,
Beauties bathing in the nude.

Turn eyes away and contemplate
The rushing waters of the sea.
There to swim and seem to feel
The water washing over me.

And that saucy, sexy swimmer,
With seduction in her eye,
Will never catch me. To be sure,
From her allure I'll quickly fly.

But, but this, this is too much,
For, as I flee your woman's charms,
I find, by gum, that I've swum
Into another trollop's arms.

Stop! Stop! The scene must change:
Bring on the golden daffodils.
But, Christ, who is this naked Jane
Who trips across the vales and hills?

The Outrageous Poems of Krunchie Killeen

What now? What now? What can I do?
More literature I'll call to mind...
Now, here, at last, is a solution,
In certain words of Oscar Wilde.

Against all the resources of the mind
Temptation doesn't yield a whit.
The only way to end temptation,
Wilde says, is to yield to it.

DO YOU YEN FOR A FEEL

(I noticed that some old men in a nursing home had delusions about getting off with the nurses)

Do you yen for a feel,
Though you're old and grey?
Do you yen for a feel,
When your wife's gone away?
Do you yen for a feel
At the break of the day,
Like a Hound with your horn
In the morning?

I met the nurse the other day
At the tight place on the stair.
I reached out my hand to touch her arse;
I did, I do declare.
And I said to her, "Me darling,
Come with me to my room".
She said for me to go ahead
And she'd follow after, soon.
She did. She followed after me,
And she tucked me into bed;
But she didn't leap in beside me;
She sedated me instead.

Do you yen for a feel,
Though you're old and grey?

The Outrageous Poems of Krunchie Killeen

Do you yen for a feel,
When your wife's far away?
Do you yen for a feel
At the break of the day,
Like a Hound with your horn
In the morning?

Sometimes, when there are visitors,
They leave the door ajar.
I slipped out surreptitiously
And made for Murphy's bar.
But the matron hollered after me,
"How did you get out?"
I said, "Me darling, come along with me
For a creamy pint of stout".
She took me firmly by the arm
And she led me back inside,
And, instead of a creamy pint, I got
A jab in the behind.

Yes, I yen for a feel,
Though I'm old and grey.
I yen for a feel,
Now my wife's far away.
Yes, I yen for a feel
At the break of the day,
Like a Hound with my horn
In the morning.

OBSESSED

My mind is obsessed with painting.
All night and all day long
I ponder the possibilities
Of composition and form.

I ponder my subject reclining
On sheets of silky black,
And command her pale, contrasting tones
Into my artefact.

I ponder my subject wearing
A brilliant scarlet gown,
And pose her semi-naked,
As she slips it gently down.

I ponder my subject flaunting
Her body fully nude,
And maintain an artistic frame of mind,
Objective, never lewd.

From an artistic frame of mind
I dwell on her curves and lines,
Reviewing a thousand poses
Her charms to maximise.

The Outrageous Poems of Krunchie Killeen

I'll pose my subject lying
Stretched out on the bed,
And bid her smile out softly
Through lips a gentle red.

My mind is composing pictures
Of every part you can name.
Imagine this stunning picture:
Two tits within a frame.

Yes, my mind is obsessed
With painting.

THE DANCE IN THE VILLAGE HALL

Tis well that I remember
The dance in the village hall,
Where the boys and girls assembled
Along each opposite wall;

And we stood there filled with tension,
As the band played on and on,
And its sentimental numbers
Re-echoed round the hall;

And, when the pubs all emptied,
The bowsies hit the scene;
There was pushing; there was shoving,
And the air, it reeked of beer;

And then, suddenly, it happened,
Like an army on attack,
The line of lads fell forward
Upon the female pack.

You were my choice, my darling,
And I nearly dropped stone dead,
When you raised your eyes to heaven,
And coldly shook your head.

The Outrageous Poems of Krunchie Killeen

You were as sweet as apple blossom,
As pure as the driven snow,
And why you danced with Bluebeard
Is a thing I'll never know.

For, yes, a bleary bluebeard
Danced and held you tight,
And your eyes closed in surrender:
You gave in without a fight.

Well, lurching was forbidden,
Said a notice on the wall.
I complained him to the bouncer.
He was thrown out of the hall.

My disgust and disappointment,
When you followed him outside.
O, the wild imaginations
Of my tormented mind!

I recall you went to England
A short while after that,
But we started going together
After you came back.

Yes, we started going together,
And my heart near burst with pride,
The day that we got married
And you became my bride.

The Outrageous Poems of Krunchie Killeen

Now, you treat me like a doormat;
You lacerate me with your tongue,
Your words all laced with acid,
Dreadful poison, every one.

So, I'm heading for the pub now
To drink a rake of beer,
After which I'll hit the disco
And shift a young colleen.

NAIROBI ZOO

You may not believe this story;
But I assure you it is true.
It's about the time I went
To visit Nairobi Zoo.

I observed a busload of children
Pull up and disembark.
The astonishment at what met them
Soon stopped all their talk.

Their eyes opened wide
At the fantastic sight they saw.
They stood around and stared
In wonder and in awe.

Their teachers, so embarrassed,
Tried to hurry them away;
But they weren't easily moved,
And all wished to stay.

Now, it was not the monkeys
That they were so wowed to see,
Nor the lions or leopards or buffaloes:
Oh no! It was me!

The Outrageous Poems of Krunchie Killeen

Yes, in astonishment they stood around
And stared and stared and stared
At this white man with snow-white hair
And remarkable white beard.

I really should have booked a cage
And charged a fee to show my face.

The Outrageous Poems of Krunchie Killeen

SILVER WEDDING

It was a mistake from the start,
For head was over-ruled by heart.
But was it heart, or lower still?
Was it lust instructed will?

Whate'er the locus, the emotion
Filled me like a noxious potion
In a stupor to embark
Upon a voyage in the dark;

To sail out upon an unknown sea
And there entrust my destiny.
I thought, perhaps, I had control,
This voyage and vessel be my own,

To steer by chart upon a course
Of which my wondrous brain be source.
That plan was vain, not on that crew
Was even one my will to do,

And soon my every act and deed
By outside forces were decreed,
So that I cried out to the wind,
"O for one sole moment mine!"

The Outrageous Poems of Krunchie Killeen

The answer came in thunderous boom:
"'Twas thou thyself that chose this doom,
To dedicate thy middle life
To years of trouble and of strife

"And chaos and tumult and disorder,
As on this luna sea you wander.
Such years are promised twenty-five,
Before some solace may arrive,

"For then thou may'st beat thy chest,
Shouting 'Offspring leave the nest;
Too long your whim has steered my course
Henceforth my own will be its source.'"

"Then, shall my life be mine once more
When offspring fly to foreign shore?"
Again the thunderous answer roars:
"No, never more. No, never more."

CORRAKIT
(From the Irish)

Lonely the homes of Corrakit;
Miserable its men and women.
They have neither joy nor wit,
And hate to spend a shillin'.

There is no music in their homes,
No harp, or flute, or fiddle.
To travelling bards they close their doors,
Disdainful and uncivil.

They pout and pray and wish to be
Alone in their misery.

UNDER THIS HARD HEADSTONE
(From the Irish, "Faoi Lár na Leice Seo)

Under this hard headstone
A grim, fat monster lies,
In death as in life
Universally despised.

In front of this hard headstone,
If you kneel to pray,
Let your prayer be, "Thank you, Lord,
That this monster's in the clay."

THE CIVIL SERVANT

The look of astonishment
Upon a person's face,
When he finds a civil servant
Has a human trait.

Some civil servants don't;
Some civil servants do.
Some actually are human.
Yes: there are a few.

THE NEW DAUGHTER OF HOULIHAN

(After W. B. Yeats' *Red Hanrahan's Song about Ireland*)

Hoods laced tight, and eyes asquint against the
    blowing sand,
We brave the storm to walk on Cummin strand.
Wow! That old tree just broke in two and half has
    taken flight,
Then crashed and tumbled like a broken kite.
Great Scott! This storm could lift you off your feet
And toss you around like a piece of tumbleweed.

Let us, then, retreat again to our solid cabin, where
In two ticks we'll have blown the fire aflame,
Drawn a cork, boiled a kettle,
Nestled, comfy, on the settle,
And, over steaming cups of mulled red wine,
I'll watch the fire's flames dancing in your eyes.

Was that a clap of thunder? Yes! and now it rolls
From Knocknarea's great cloud cap down across the
    stones.
Be not alarmed, but calmly stretch out on the bed
And let my magic hands instead
With aromatic oils your languid body treat,
Until at length I'll bend low and kiss your scented
    feet.

The Outrageous Poems of Krunchie Killeen

A sudden burst of thundery rain
Clatters and bangs against the window pane
And we can even hear the stream in torrents roar
For by now the yellow pool on Clooth has overflown.
The storm inside our bodies to new heights has
       climbed
As I place the tall white candle inside the holy shrine.

MAYO IN JULY

In Mayo, July is often like November:
Dark Clouds all day obliterate the sun;
A storm marauds across the uncut meadows,
And the mood of every living thing is glum.

The rain falls down in solid sheets of water;
The rivers and the streams are all in flood;
The turf we cut washed back into the bog, sir,
And the soggy cows are ankle deep in mud.

In the pub the farmers talk about the weather,
As they lower pint after pint after pint of beer.
There's nothing else to do, but come together
And drink, as they wait in vain for the rain to clear.

Visitors there are coaxed, cajoled and led
To drink all night and spend the day in bed.

HE DOESN'T LOVE ME ANY MORE

She said, "He doesn't love me any more,
Although he swears sweet nothings as before
And smothers me with kindness, even more,
My lover doesn't love me anymore,

She said, "He doesn't love me now, the bastard.
He will not take Viagra, though I asked it;
Now there is no content in his casket;
My fucker's just gone fifty, but he's past it.

DILLY'S DIET

Dilly being overweight
Caused her doctor her to berate:
"If you lose a few pounds,
You're heart will be sound
And your figure will really be great."

But now Dilly's gone so thin,
She's nothing but bone and skin.
The fact of the matter,
Her figure, when fatter,
Was more to my fanciful whim.

Dilly One was a wee bit fat;
Dilly Two is too thin, it's a fact.
Mix both together
To make a half measure:
I tell you, I'd really love that.

The Outrageous Poems of Krunchie Killeen

ONE TEA BAG

One tea bag can furnish
Many cups of tea.
That they waste so many
Is a cause of concern to me.

Too often I see them
Throw the bag away,
After it has furnished
A single cup of tay.

Please take the tea bag out
After a count of two;
And hang it up to dry
Like civil servants do.

Hang it up and use it
At the next tea break:
And see how many cups
One tea bag can make.

Don't leave the tea bag in
Till the tea is thick as tar.
Dip it in and take it out
For a better cup by far.

The Outrageous Poems of Krunchie Killeen

Then you can enjoy that bag,
Again and again.
Green Label, I have found,
Can make up to ten.

And, when the flavour's all used up,
Still don't let it go.
Assign it to the compost heap
To help your garden grow.

The Outrageous Poems of Krunchie Killeen

HOME COMPUTERS

Home computers were devised
By a fellow of subversive frame of mind:
His object, within the home,
To create conditions of revolt.
The machine would be a teenage tool
To make middle aged dad feel a fool.

Terms like "ROM" and "RAM" and "Bus"
That don't mean anything to us
Would soon enriddle teenage chat,
Confirm the generation gap,
Make kids feel the power of knowledge
And see their dads as useless fossils.

Wisdom, they would soon believe
Is only proper to the teens,
Which hitherto was deemed to reign
Inside their know-all father's brain.
And so, insidiously, is blown
Authority within the home.

But revolution, now as ever,
Will fail, for those in power are clever

The Outrageous Poems of Krunchie Killeen

At turning tables, for, indeed,
In revolts that seemingly succeed,
Mostly the incoming power
Is the self same class that ruled before.

Now every night in every 'tech
I'll tell you what you can expect -
Middle-aged dads with furrowed brow
Learning all there is to know
About these things, and, by this means,
Restoring power o'er their teens.

And, yes, the last laugh will be ours,
For computers will enlarge our powers.
Those office "chicks" whom we heard speak
About us as "that old creep"
Will learn that we can get along
Without them, now that, for a song,

We can have computers do accounts
And rattle all those letters out.
One girl now is all we'll need;
You can guess, of course, which one we'll keep:
That lissom lass we'd love to lay
To whom we heard the others say,

The Outrageous Poems of Krunchie Killeen

"How can you fancy that old creep,"
For middle-aged revenge is sweet.
And when school leavers ask for jobs,
We'll simply tell them to get lost.
So, son, you may be brave and slim,
And I pot-bellied with lewd grin,

But here's a saying you should take in:
You are out and I am in.
No work for you, more cash for me,
We call this productivity.
The computer's function thus is stated:
Power to the Middle Aged.

THE SECOND SIXTY-FIVE

The natural human life-span is 130 years, or 150, if, according to Dr Karach MD, we practice Oil Pulling: see www.oilpulling.com.

Well, at the age of sixty five,
Says you, I'm lucky to be alive.
But the odds are very good today
A second sixty five will come my way.

So, get up on your feet and share my joy.
And Jump around like a bouncy boy.
And Stamp your feet and laugh and shout
And throw your arms and legs about.
Aren't we lucky to be alive
To enjoy the second sixty five?

Well, when my life was just begun,
The odds were a billion or so to one
That I wouldn't survive till half this age:
Now look at me bouncing around the stage.

So, get up on your feet and share my joy.
And Jump around like a bouncy boy.
And Stamp your feet and laugh and shout
And throw your arms and legs about.
Aren't we lucky to be alive
To enjoy the second sixty five?

The Outrageous Poems of Krunchie Killeen

The odds were then I'd be carried off
By measles or the whooping cough,
Or a drunken driver in an Austin car;
But I wasn't and I've done alright so far.

So, get up on your feet and share my joy.
And Jump around like a bouncy boy.
And Stamp your feet and laugh and shout
And throw your arms and legs about.
Aren't we lucky to be alive
To enjoy the second sixty five?

Now, what are the odds from here on in
That the whooping cough will do me in?
Not very great, and reduced by far
Is the risk I'll be caught by an Austin car.

So, get up on your feet and share my joy.
And Jump around like a bouncy boy.
And Stamp your feet and laugh and shout
And throw your arms and legs about.
Aren't we lucky to be alive
To enjoy the second sixty five?

The odds are good that I'll survive
Indeed another sixty five.
No need to heed the prophets of doom:
To celebrate, dance around the room.

The Outrageous Poems of Krunchie Killeen

So, get up on your feet and share my joy.
And Jump around like a bouncy boy.
And Stamp your feet and laugh and shout
And throw your arms and legs about.
Aren't we lucky to be alive
To enjoy the second sixty five?

HALLOWE'EN

(At Hallowe'en, or rather Samhain, the night of the full moon half way between the Autumn Equinox and the Winter Solstice, the souls of the dead return to inhabit the bodies of newly-conceived infants, but might stay to haunt your home if you have not provided a feast outside. You might have thought the apples were knocked by the wind, but no).

Hey, did you hear
Grandad and his gang
Raid the orchard –
To leave
Half their loot
Half-eaten on the ground,

Then rush
To the bonfire
To dance their crazy dance,
Leaping high
To every flicker
Of the Flame,

And shout
'Their ribald refrain:
"What we want
What we want
What we want
Is to be born again,"

The Outrageous Poems of Krunchie Killeen

And whisper
In the ear of moon-struck women
To do the deed
With an upstanding man
And make a fertile egg
To invade
And lodge their soul,

Even while the Pooka
Raced around
Fouling all the berries
We should have picked
Ere now?

Or did you fail
To leave an outdoor feast,
Or light
Your bonfire
On the wrong night,
For they come,
Not on Church-night,
But on the night
Of the moon?

Then, did you hear
Noises
Late at night
In your larder?
It is they!

The Outrageous Poems of Krunchie Killeen

Then, open wide your door
At sunset,
And ask them to leave,
For, the longer they linger,
The more likely are they
To make your house
Their home.

THE ROWAN AT AUTUMN

Oh, Ellie Rowan,
Half-naked now,
Your limbs show through
Your scarlet gown.

With one blow
And shake, soon
All the rest
Will tumble down.

Then you'll stand stark
To all the men
Til young Bride in Spring
Clothe you again.

JACUZZI

I wonder wot 'appened to my sperms
W'en I wanked in the Jacuzzi.
Did the chlorine zap them right there and then
Or did they live to search out Jill or Suzy?

What is the lifespan of spermatozoa
Ejaculated in water?
If a lady bathed after me,
Could I now have a son or a daughter?

The finny fishes in the sea
Do this all the time,
Which accounts for all the baby fishies
Brimming in the brine.

Is there now somewhere a virgin,
Amazed at her condition,
Attributing to the angels
My miraculous addition?

SWINGING IN THE CHOIR
(A fictional choir of course)

The swinging began
When the choir went on tour,
Each Soprano and Alto
Already a whore
When we sang for the Pope
In Rome.

Father McCarthy
Was at it a lot.
We found he was both
A sod and a sot.
With no altar-boys,
Every Tenor he tried.
With respect for the cloth
Each one complied
And welcomed him into
The fold.

As we headed for home
We swore to stay mum,
But never forsake
What we had begun.

Choir swings every week
On each Thursday night

The Outrageous Poems of Krunchie Killeen

Leaving our spouses
At home.

Avoiding attachment,
It's best, so we found,
To constantly pass
The partners around.
We hope to continue,
For swinging is fun,
For ever and ever,
Amen.

The Outrageous Poems of Krunchie Killeen

RESOLUTION

On this, the first of January,
Let each man raise his beer
And make a solemn resolution
For the coming year.

Resolve not rash, but wisely;
The world is in a mess.
To make it a happier place
We all must do our best.

Now, you could battle poverty,
But of this you can be sure,
The rich will get still richer
And the poor ones will stay poor.

Well, you could join the Legion
And wage a war on sin;
But you'd only break your fecking heart
In a cause you know can't win.

You could, of course, campaign for peace
And try to stop the bombs;
But face the truth, whatever you do,
The troubles will still go on.

The Outrageous Poems of Krunchie Killeen

Inflation, strife, injustice,
Disasters and pollution:
The world is full of problems, friend,
For which you've no solution.

Then, is there nothing you can do,
But worry all day long
About the world's misfortunes
And how everything's gone wrong?

If you're to improve the world,
There's but one place to start:
Eliminate the misery
Inside in your own heart.

So, let's join the drinking brotherhood,
Who night by night get pissed,
And banish misfortune
With Bacchanalian bliss.

(The "Legion" referred to is the Legion of Mary, an organisation devoted to promoting moral well-being).

The Outrageous Poems of Krunchie Killeen

PISTACHIOS

Achios is his name,
But on Saturday night he became
      Pistachios.

After a row on the street,
A man he just happened to meet
      Stitched Achios.

He's the sexiest man in the world,
So, happy, indeed, is the girl
      Who kissed Achios.

His wife is as strong as a man.
She, once, with a frying pan
      Hit Achios.

So, languishing now in jail,
He wonders how he will explain
      His sitachios.

Of course, Achios is a Greek,
With tufts of hair on his cheek
      And mistachios.

Achios has a ship.
There's a figure carved out on the tip
      With titachios.

The Outrageous Poems of Krunchie Killeen

His mother, who stayed living at home,
When Achios set out to roam,
      Missed Achios.

But they say his father did not,
For he, when his son was a tot,
      Ditched Achios.

Whatever, whoever to blame,
Now he rues the night he became
      Pistachios.

THE THRUSH

I believe it was a thrush that woke me up at dawn,
although I never seemed to hear it during the day.

I curse and swear to hear
The thrush sing at dawn.
Push off, you little fecker,
I hate your blasted song.

I pull the wretched blanket
Up around my ears;
But still your throbbing arias
My tender eardrums pierce.

Where are you
At the afternoon of the day,
When I sit in the conservatory
With my cup of tay?

The robin comes to call me
To the garden,
And the blackbird sings his heart out
To his darling.

But all day long
Your voice is dormant.
No doubt resting
For a dawn performance.

The Outrageous Poems of Krunchie Killeen

Since you persist in this,
I cry out, and beg
The mad and cackling magpies
To hack your sky-blue egg

And harass you
Until you fly away
To the plains of Africa,
Where they dawn-rise anyway.

PADDY MACARONI

On the appointment of Giovanni Trapatoni as manager of the Irish soccer team

The spud has been abandoned here:
We're eating macaroni.
Cast off your gloom, be of good cheer
And follow Trapattoni.
Cast off your gloom; be of good cheer;
Our day of glory's coming near;
To face the foe we have no fear
With Giovanni Trapattoni.

Let's celebrate our new-born cheer
With Paddy Trapattoni.
With Jack the Lad we had a beer
Now it's wine and macaroni.
And now, when we go out to dine,
We'll all shout, "Macaroni's fine"
And a bottle of Bardolino wine
To toast Don Trapattoni.

We believe that we can match the best
With Paddy Trapattoni.
And we'll grow hairs upon our chest
By eating macaroni.
Bang the bowran, beat the drum;
The world will know our hour is come.
We'll don the green, for everyone
Will follow Trapattoni.

ITALIANS

I don't think they work in Italy:
It is far too hot.
They loll around in languid mode,
Drink wine, and talk a lot.

And they sing "O Solo Mio,"
Morning, noon and night;
And, every time they sing it,
They sing it with delight.

I'm glad they're not in Ireland,
Where soon they'd learn to sing
Of sorrow and betrayal,
And make a moan out of everything.

I'm glad they're not in Ireland,
Where, if they winked, or pinched an ass,
They'd find themselves up before
A Tribunal very fast.

Their chatter sounds like music,
Which inspires me to make this plea:
Let's swap our Anglo-Saxon tongue
For the lingua of Italy.

The Outrageous Poems of Krunchie Killeen

And, over Dublin City,
Let's build a great glass dome,
Turn Winter into Summer,
And loll around like lads in Rome.

The Outrageous Poems of Krunchie Killeen

OBAMA'S LIKE MY FATHER

O'Bama's like my father:
He has an Irish name.
They call him "Barrack" in America,
But it's "Paurick" just the same.

O'Bama's like my father:
He lays down the Law.
We must be related, for
He has dad's righteous jaw.

Every time he speaks,
His command is clear.
There is no room for doubt
In the minds of those who hear.

How wonderful, the media cries:
America has a voice!
Una duce, una voce:
So let us rejoice.

Let difference of opinion
Now be set aside;
Let the world move forward
With unity and pride.

The Outrageous Poems of Krunchie Killeen

Father, when you bid me
Tread the rightful path,
Are there not many such,
I would answer back.

I would answer back,
Only that I fear
That I would get another
Clip on the ear.

Father, when you tell me
To lie is to sin,
I would answer that your truth
Of many is but one.

Obama's like my father:
He displays no doubt;
But whether he is always right
We still must figure out.

LEWINSKY

Every married man would like
A Lewinsky in his office;
And, I suggest, a clever wife
Will turn this to her profit.

She knows from that nervous smile
That spreads across a husband's face
That some sort of surreptitious joys
Engage her happy mate.

She doesn't fly into a rage,
Demanding explanations;
But showers him with compliments
And loving declarations.

She knows a guilty husband will
Double his attention;
So can derive more quality time
Because of his attrition.

She doesn't tell him that she knows,
And knows not if he knows
She knows, or if he knows she knows
He knows she knows.

The Outrageous Poems of Krunchie Killeen

In her mind she keeps a quiet account
Of favours that she's owed,
And, at a whim, will often bid him
Kiss her tacky toes.

So, a married woman can benefit from
A Lewinsky in the office,
And, so long as it is not let out,
Can turn it to her profit.

THE DAWNING OF THE DAY
(From the Irish)

One morning early, I set out by Killarney's Lake so fair.
The dew was sparkling on the grass and sunlight warmed the air.
The blooms were bursting from the bough, as it was the month of May,
And a mystery girl walked by my side, at the Dawning of the Day.

She wore no cap; she wore no cloak, my darling from the sky.
Her golden hair was all she wore, and the twinkle in her eye.
There was beauty in her every pore and sprightly was her stride,
And stepping out beside her, I was joyful and alive.

The robin sang on every side, the blackbird and the dove,
And, on the lake, the ducks and drake played out their game of love.
The pulsating earth was mating with the very sky above,
And my heart sang out inside my breast as by the lake we roved.

PASSIVE RESISTANCE

I sit before the Master
In silent prayer.

I offer no answer;
But close my ear.

I will not tend his garden,
His table or his chair.

I will not serve his household,
His agents or his care.

Without my consent, he can be
No master of me.

The Outrageous Poems of Krunchie Killeen

SEE CRETARY GENTS

Dag's Hammer's Cold,
Wanky Moon.
You Shan't be so bold,
I assume.

Put the Coffee On, On
For Tricky Lee;
But Have Your Perry Stay
Colour of the tea.

Whatever Hurt Walt, Time
Will Tell.
Till then But Rest: But Rest
Gaily in your cell.

(Dag Hammarskjold, Ban Ki-moon, U Thant, Kofi Annan, Trigve Lee, Javier Peres de Cuellar, Kurt Waldheim, Boutros Boutros Ghali)

JASPER, JASPER

Jasper, Jasper, in the sky,
Why do you make so many die?
Tsunami, earthquake, flood and storm:
Why cause such harm?

Krunchie, Krunchie, you ought to know,
With the intellect on man bestowed:
It's sort of true what you have learned, son;
In Me, there are three disparate Persons.

While the First one's job is to create,
And the job of the Second is to sustain,
The Third Person's function is to destroy,
So that the First can start again, my boy.

Jasper, Jasper, such distress!
The world is in a fearsome mess
Because your creatures kill and maim:
But are you not yourself to blame?

Krunchie, Krunchie, that's my plan,
For all of nature, not just man.
Take the birds you've been observing
Hopping around your winter garden.

The female blackbird you observed
Chases off the other birds.

The Outrageous Poems of Krunchie Killeen

Although you've left enough for all,
Instead of sharing, she makes war.

And then she makes sure her man
Stays true to her to mind her clan,
While, surreptitiously, she lets
A stranger fertilise her eggs.

O yes, the strongest will survive,
And the one most cunning to connive.
To make diversity, my solution
Is found in the laws of evolution.

This is how My plan's progressed:
By violence and lies and sex.
Each creature promoting self and seed
By covetousness and by greed.

So, when all is said and done,
Remember, my other name is Krumm.

Note: Jasper is from the Irish *Dia* ("Ja") *Spéir'* ("Sper"), meaning "God of the Sky." "Krumm" is *Crom Cruach* – pronounce "Krumm Kroo-akh" – Celtic god of self-interest.

DUBLIN CAN BE HEAVEN

"Dublin can be Heaven:"
But it will cost you more
Than the price that you would pay
In Bankok or Bangalore.

"Coffey at eleven!"
I remember when
We could afford it every day,
But a lot has changed since then.

"A stroll in Stephen's Green:"
Wear your scarf and woolly hat,
And carry an umbrella:
You'll probably need that.

"Grafton Street's a Wonderland:"
True, now that the miniskirt's in fashion!
But the diamonds in the lady's eyes
May put you back on rations.

The Outrageous Poems of Krunchie Killeen

MY LAST GLASS OF WINE

I remember my last
Glass of wine,
Fulsome, flavoursome,
Sublime,

And the feeling
That ensued,
Mellow, restful,
Peace imbued.

Relaxing in
My easy chair,
My heart and mind
Knew no care.

Ah, my soul!
Glass of wine!
I remember,
Mood sublime.

And so I raise
To my lip
Another glass
For fulsome sip.

The Outrageous Poems of Krunchie Killeen

STARING EYES

(My reflection in the mirror reminded me of the staring effigies of Padre Pio and other saints in the souvenir shops in Knock).

I have the staring eyes
      And grim expression
Of a true-born saint.

I have deep concern
      And commiseration
For all of those who aint.

It hurts me now
      To think about
Young ones engaged in sin.

I pray each day
      They get the grace
To reel their passions in.

O dear, o dear,
      The shameless way
They laugh and show their wares.

What will become
      Of God's great world,
When this lot comes of age?

The Outrageous Poems of Krunchie Killeen

I love to think
     They will engage
In penance and in prayer,

Forsake this phase of
     Rakishness
And take on board life's cares.

I hope that
     By the end they all
Will have learned life's lesson,

And approach their God
     With staring eyes
And a grim expression.

The Outrageous Poems of Krunchie Killeen

HOUR ON A BEAN

Air: Chorus of the Irish National Anthem. Next time you are at an Irish football match, sing along with these words. Nobody will know the difference!

She on a fee on a fall,
A toffee: ya'll a caring?
Been there slew;
Heard e'en the Ronnie cooing.

Fee vote, face-hair,
Shan't hear our chin, sir, faster.
Knee hog-fur,
Faint here on'? Naw, faint drawl!

Un-knocked, a hames,
Savannah bale;
Leg an' a gale,
Con boss, no sale.

Leg on knee, as rake,
Fee law-whack, nappy lair.
Show Liv, Connie,
Hour on a Bean!

The Outrageous Poems of Krunchie Killeen

Index

PREFACE TO THE 3RD EDITION	3
JUNIRA NATIONS	4
TIT SHAKING	6
FEMALE MODES OF DRESS (OR THE MINISKIRT)	8
CAT	12
CATERPILLAR	13
PADDY BALONEY	14
WRITING ABOUT YOU	16
GARDEN OF FLOWERS	18
CHRISTMAS WHEN	19
GANDHI'S KNELL	20
THE WITCH	22
COLM CILLE AT LOCH NESS	26
FRANKIE WANKIE	28
APPROACHING TWENTY	30
TWENTY-ONE (PUT YOUR MINISKIRT ON)	31
THE BOURGEOISIE	33
TYPING SECTION	38
JOAN MAGUIRE	39
TRAIN TO HELL	41
RAFTERY THE POET	44
BRIAN BORU'S FEASTING	46
BRIAN BORU'S FEASTING	46
HIMALAYAN LONGEVITY	49
LILY WHITE BREAST	51
RETIREMENT SONG	53
THE HERO	55
STATUE	56
WORMS	58
SPARE A THOUGHT	60

The Outrageous Poems of Krunchie Killeen

THE GREAT GOD PAN	62
JIMMY LOVES MARY	64
BOOKS	65
IN SLATTERY'S	66
KRUNCHIE AND MILADY	68
WOMAN'S DESIRE	73
THE DA	74
THE GREAT SIX - O	77
MY GARDEN	79
GOOD MORNING	80
SNOW WHITE	81
VACANT MOOD	83
DO YOU YEN FOR A FEEL	86
OBSESSED	88
THE DANCE IN THE VILLAGE HALL	90
NAIROBI ZOO	93
SILVER WEDDING	95
CORRAKIT	97
UNDER THIS HARD HEADSTONE	98
THE CIVIL SERVANT	99
THE NEW DAUGHTER OF HOULIHAN	100
MAYO IN JULY	102
HE DOESN'T LOVE ME ANY MORE	103
DILLY'S DIET	104
ONE TEA BAG	105
HOME COMPUTERS	107
THE SECOND SIXTY-FIVE	110
HALLOWE'EN	113
THE ROWAN AT AUTUMN	116
JACUZZI	117
SWINGING IN THE CHOIR	118
RESOLUTION	120
PISTACHIOS	122

The Outrageous Poems of Krunchie Killeen

THE THRUSH	**124**
PADDY MACARONI	**126**
ITALIANS	**127**
OBAMA'S LIKE MY FATHER	**129**
LEWINSKY	**131**
THE DAWNING OF THE DAY	**133**
PASSIVE RESISTANCE	**134**
SEE CRETARY GENTS	**135**
JASPER, JASPER	**136**
DUBLIN CAN BE HEAVEN	**138**
MY LAST GLASS OF WINE	**139**
STARING EYES	**140**
THE AUTHOR	**146**

The Outrageous Poems of Krunchie Killeen

THE AUTHOR

"Krunchie Killeen" is a pseudonym of Proinnsias Ó Cillín ("Francis Killeen" in English).

He started writing poems when he was seven years old, his first a lampoon of a classmate who had devised a war-game played with pencil and paper, which was so constrained that his pal always had to win. Krunchie (in amused frustration) decided to write a poem (contained in this volume) making a mockery of the project.

He wrote lyrical, pensive and philosophical poems, but found there was no audience except for the outrageous and comical ones, usually recited to a live audience.

One Christmas he and his two brothers were given a tin whistle each, but no lessons. At that age, finding it difficult to capture airs by ear or from sheet-music, Krunchie made up his own tunes, some of which had words, such as:

> "O mystic moon, overhead,
> Some of your magic on us shed …"

and:

> "There's a man with a can
> With an old Billy Can
> And he lives all his life
> > By the road …"

and, in Irish:

> "Ó tóg mo lámh, a ghrá mo chléibh,
> Is fan, ó fan, a rún, lem' thaobh …"

("'O take my hand, love of my chest, and stay, my darling, by my side …"

The Outrageous Poems of Krunchie Killeen

Mrs Breen, next door, is reported to have said: "You always know when Krunchie is at home, because you will hear the tin whistle blowing."

Krunchie's sister, Margaret, was born when he was ten, and Krunchie, in his turn rocking the cradle, composed his own lullaby for the baby:

> "The dreary night is drawing near,
> So go to sleep my baby dear …"

Krunchie obtained qualifications in Law (BL First Class Honours) and Information Technology (M Sc for his thesis *"A Model for Land Registration in the Information Age"*) and spent many years as a lawyer in the employment of the Irish Civil Service, mostly in the Land Registry in Dublin, as well as a subsequent career as Land Registration Consultant. He has been a member of Irish Language organisations, a Jurist-Linguist, a Gaeltacht Official, an Examiner of Titles, a Community Activist, an artist and Chairman of Art Groups, founder of Peoples Art Dublin, pub performer and amateur actor, and a University Lecturer.

Besides his Outrageous Poems, Krunchie has written a number of other books on disparate subjects, available now or soon on Amazon:

- **Simplified Land Titling** (encapsulating his insights from 45 alert years in Land Registration and his study of Information Technology) offers a comprehensive and universal solution to land-ownership problems, including a secure title for billions of owners who now lack documentary title;

- **Transport 21 Hundred** describes a driverless and practical transport system dreamed up by him with zero carbon emissions, high speed, low-cost, accident-free, automatically routed, door-to-door transit across the globe;

- **KIM: Krunchie's Input Method**, a highly intuitive keyboard that fits on a shirt-button, to completely replace the QWERTY keyboard;

- **Infinity Nonsense**, a refutation, inter alia, of the "transfinite" of Georg Cantor and "non-computable numbers" of Alan Turing;

- **The Sayings of Frank**, a collection of the precepts of his father, Frank Killeen, who believed in honesty and discipline;

- **Fables for Our Times**, which take a sceptical view of aspects of public affairs.

He plays with the Invincibles and reads patriotic scripts on the CD **"The Graves of Glasnevin,"** available at:

https://shop.glasnevintrust.ie/products/the-clareville-invincibles-graves-of-glasnevin.

He keeps a blog at https://killeensinfo.blogspot.ie and www.killeens.info.

Made in the USA
Columbia, SC
28 June 2017